Explode The Co… 2nd Edition …½

Phonics review and reinforcement

Nancy Hall • Rena Price

Ziggy sells polka dot pants.

EDUCATORS PUBLISHING SERVICE
Cambridge and Toronto

Cover art: Hugh Price
Text illustrations: Kelly Kennedy

Printed in Mayfield, PA, in April 2021
ISBN 978-0-8388-7813-2

8 9 10 PAH 24 23 22 21

CONTENTS

Lesson 1

-all says /all/ as in b*all*.
-alk says /awk/ as in w*alk*.

Read, write, and ◯ it.

bald bald			
talk			
hallway			
waterfall			
smallest			
walnuts			
baseball			

( ) the word that matches the picture.

	Spell.				Write.
	over	om	alls	let	______________
	snee	snow	dell	ball	______________
	malt	salt	ed	end	______________
	side	see	walk	talk	______________
	call	cold	ish	ing	______________
	seal	wal	nuts	rus	______________
	wal	mal	let	ed	______________

Yes or no?

	Yes	No
Can we talk over plans in the hallway?	☐	☐
Is it easy to go shopping at a mall?	☐	☐
Can a sidewalk run sideways?	☐	☐
Does a walrus like to munch salted peanuts?	☐	☐
Do you want to walk into that wall?	☐	☐
Does a bald eagle need a wig in a snowfall?	☐	☐
Do you recall what you read in an almanac?	☐	☐

⬭ the word that matches the picture.

wallboard talking (washable)	balding bald eagle ballot
snowfall rainfall waterfall	bathtub baseball basement
balk bald stalk	snowball sidewalk sideways
checkerboard chalkboard checkers	instant install instep
fallout falling filling	taker talker taller

Pick the best word to finish each sentence.

salted	~~overalls~~	hallway
chalk	recall	wallet
waterfall	bald eagle	Hall of Fame

It is wise to put on overalls before weeding the beans.

The __________________ is a symbol of the U.S.

I cannot always __________________ my number facts.

Babe Ruth is a member of the Baseball __________________ .

You will get wet if you stand under a __________________ .

Peanuts taste better if they are __________________ .

It is best to keep money and snapshots in a ______________ .

X it.

The vase has fallen off the table.	☐	
Humpty has fallen off the stone wall.	☐	
Molly guzzles all of the milk.	☐	
Molly's hot rod is a gas guzzler.	☐	
Bolo is waltzing to the music.	☐	
Buster is waltzing slowly with Lola.	☐	
Salted walnuts are a tasty treat.	☐	
Sally likes to eat wheat flakes.	☐	
Omel is the tallest student in the class.	☐	
Omel is the fastest swimmer in the class.	☐	
That daredevil Leo has a close call.	☐	
Lela sits close to the chalkboard.	☐	
Kenisha cannot recall the math problem.	☐	
Kenisha installs a wall for her pony.	☐	

Write it, using a word with *-al.*

	snowball

Lesson 2

Sometimes words with *-ol* and *-ost* say /ō/ as in *c<u>old</u>* and *m<u>ost</u>*.

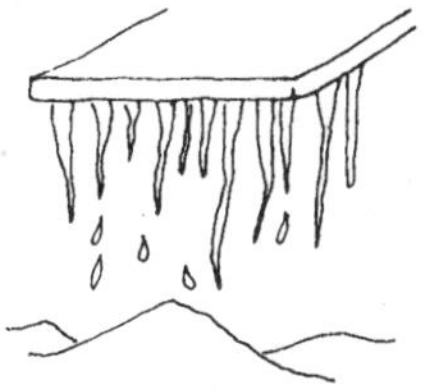

Read, write, and ⬭ it.

rolling pin ____________			
troll ____________			
cold feet ____________			
moldy ____________			
bold folks ____________			
roller skate ____________			
folders ____________		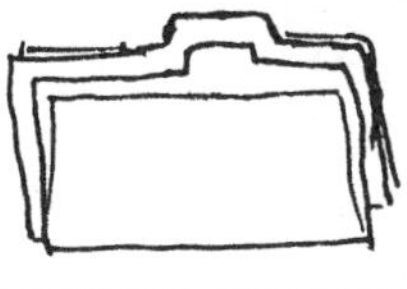	

◯ the word that matches the picture.

troll or toll?	paster or poster?
postman or posthole?	roller blades or skateboard?
coltish or coldness?	gold rush or goldfinch?
pot holder or box holder?	folktale or folk music?
trolling or stroller?	boldest or moldy?

	Spell.		Write.
	toll mol	gate dy	________
	sold scold	ing ier	________
	gold hold	fish flash	________
	past post	er haste	________
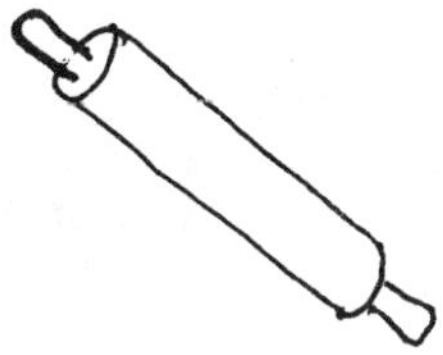	rolling hair	pin pine	________
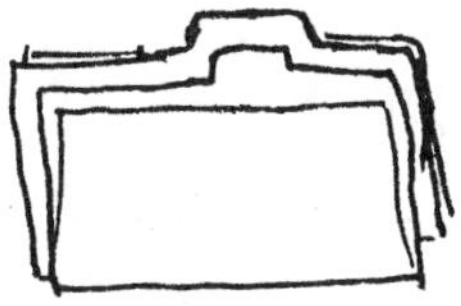	cold fold	ing ers	________
	sole stroll	er ing	________

Yes or no?

	Yes	No
Did Goldilocks miss her own bed?	☐	☐
Can you unroll a sleeping bag?	☐	☐
Will a postman ride in a stroller?	☐	☐
Do most folks play folk music?	☐	☐
Is it fun to roller skate on the sidewalk?	☐	☐
Do you need a pot holder for cold feet?	☐	☐
Is moldy cake good to eat?	☐	☐

the word that matches the picture.

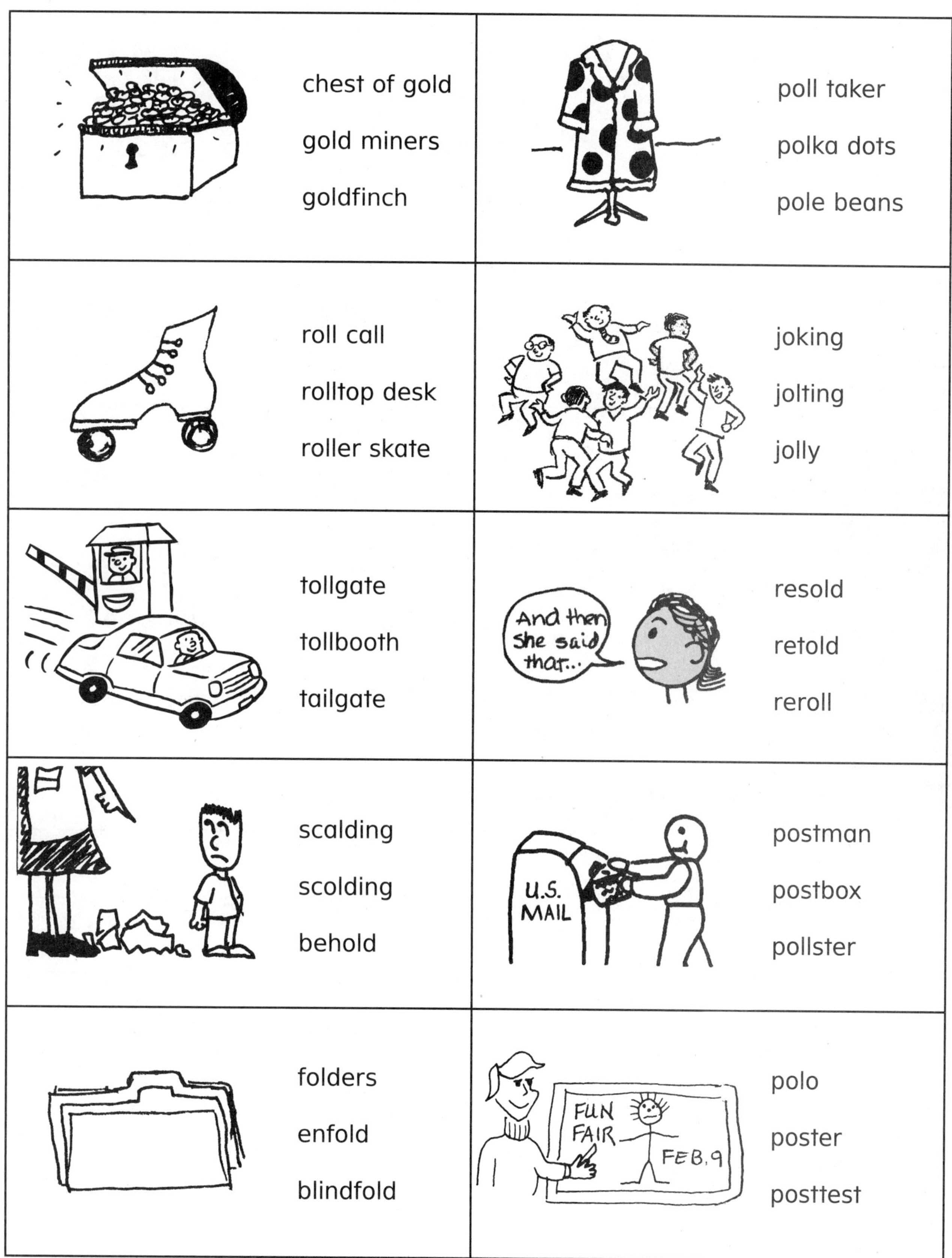

Pick the best word to finish each sentence.

troll	rolling pin	bolted
coldness	unfolded	goldenrod
poster	stroller	folder

A ____________________ is a tiny person in a fairy tale who lives in a cave.

Dad uses a ____________________ when he makes pie crust.

We carefully ____________________ the flag and put it up the pole.

When you finish the math paper, put it inside the ____________________ .

Let's paint a big ____________________ for the Fun Fair.

The baby likes to ride in the ____________________ .

Goldy shut the gate and ____________________ it.

X it.

Jo misses the tollgate but hits a post.	☐	
Miss Jo misses the postman today.	☐	
Tex holds the rolling pin over the pie.	☐	
Tilly hopes to fix the old pipes.	☐	
Tessie rolls over when I tell her to.	☐	
Les rolls up his old green backpack.	☐	
Lena holds her dog by its leash.	☐	
Lena scolds her dog for chasing a cat.	☐	
Max has a polka-dot tie.	☐	
Moxy folds the pot holder.	☐	
Bea holds a land crab on her lap.	☐	
Behold! I think I see land!	☐	
Mom fixes cold hash for the troll.	☐	
The troll fixes Mom's old hat.	☐	

Write it, using a word with *-ol* or *-ost.*

Lesson 3

Words with *-ild* and *-ind* may say /ī/ as in *ch<u>ild</u>.*

Read, write, and ◯ it.

wildest __________			
kindness __________		SAND	
poster paints __________		U.S. MAIL	
binder __________			
unsold __________			For Sale
basketball __________			
hind end __________			

◯ the word that matches the picture.

	Spell.				Write.
	un	ob	wind	sold	______
	talk	tall	set	est	______
	post	pest	man	er	______
	pre	be	hind	hand	______
	find	bind	est	er	______
	wild	water	fall	life	______
	blind	bind	fold	fill	______

Yes or no?

	Yes	No
Can you wind up a postman?	☐	☐
Can you come from behind and win?	☐	☐
Will you take your binder to class?	☐	☐
Is a walrus a blind seal?	☐	☐
Can you grind beef for meatballs?	☐	☐
Can land that is unsold be for sale?	☐	☐
Do you need a reminder to find your way home?	☐	☐

◯ the word that matches the picture.

roller coaster roller blades roll call	behind behold enfold
postcard posttest poster	fall back folktale folk song
snowball wastebasket basketball	funding finding fanning
kindling kindness mankind	lemonade lemon rind lemon tea
grinder grinding grinning	wildfire wildlife wilderness

Pick the best word to finish each sentence.

sold	binder	childless
kindness	smallest	reminder
tallest	old	wildlife

It is fun to be the ________________ player on the team.
That old shed is not ________________ yet.
Pat and Pete Wild have no kids, so they are ________________ .
Toby needs a ________________ to brush his teeth when it is bedtime.
Rachel shows much ________________ to her animals.
I can't eat this because it is too ________________ .
The class likes to read about the ________________ of Africa.

X it.

Jill's kindness pleases June.	☐	
It is unkind of June to be rude to Jill.	☐	
We remind the king not to swim alone.	☐	
The king does not mind skating alone.	☐	
Wes finds the shed is not open.	☐	
Wes finds the money he lost.	☐	
Greta has the wildest hairdo.	☐	
Greta likes to take snapshots of wildlife.	☐	
The child pulls her wagon behind her.	☐	
The wagon has a broken wheel and no handle.	☐	
Stan grinds his teeth in his sleep.	☐	
Stan is glad he did not get a salad.	☐	
Rosco likes lemon rind in his cold drink.	☐	
Rosa puts too much salt on the meatballs.	☐	

Write it, using a word with *-all, -ild,* or *-ind.*

	____________________
For Sale	____________________
	____________________
	____________________
	____________________
	____________________
	____________________

Lesson 4

Words with *x, y,* and *z.*

Read, write, and ◯ it.

pretzel ____________			
yolk ____________			
exit ____________	 EXIT		
fuzzy ____________			
explode ____________		 BERT	
zero ____________			
dozen ____________		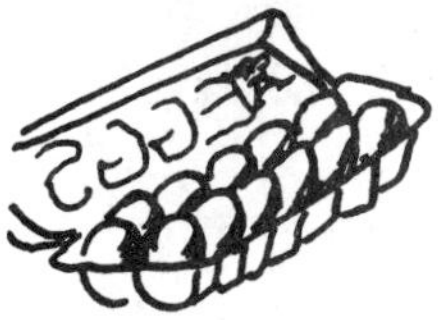	

the word that matches the picture.

	Spell.				Write.
	zip	yell	ing	ist	______________
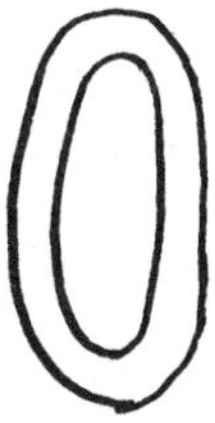	ze	zip	ro	po	______________
	ex	ze	plode	plore	______________
	zo	yo	go	yo	______________
	buzz	bus	ing	wing	______________
	yip	zip	pe	per	______________
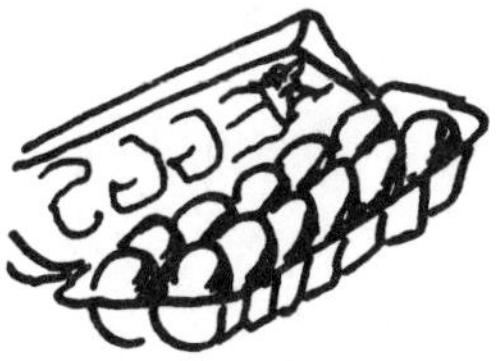	doz	zip	ping	en	______________

Yes or no?

	Yes	No
Can you hear a black fly buzzing?	☐	☐
Will you explode if you yodel?	☐	☐
Can you explain a problem?	☐	☐
Do you want to explore in the jungle?	☐	☐
Can your dog be yelping at the exit?	☐	☐
Do they play jazz at an exam?	☐	☐
Can you eat a fried egg with a yolk?	☐	☐

◯ the word that matches the picture.

yodel yolk yo-yo	exit exam extra
yelping yippee zigzagging	yellowish yellowtail yesterday
quizzing buzzing sneezing	extreme explode explain
zoo zero zipper	yummy yeast yearly
yanking yearly Yankee	02135 zip code zenith zebra

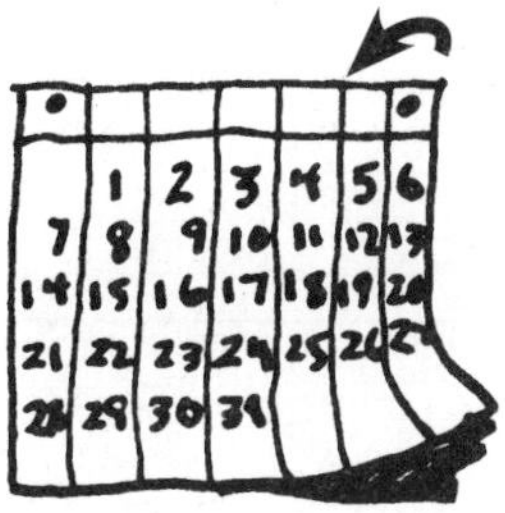

Pick the best word to finish each sentence.

yelling	zipper	exact
yo-yo	fuzzy	dozen
zero	yesterday	expect

We ____________________ that Dizzy will visit us next week.

If you find twelve eggs in a basket, you have a __________________ .

Freckles is a very ____________________ dog with long hair.

Coco is ____________________ for his sister to come to lunch.

The day before today was ____________________ .

A toy that rolls back and forth on a string is a ____________________ .

The seam of the old jacket was stuck in the ____________________ .

X it.

Franny will squeeze the red-hot peppers. ☐ The hot pepper makes Fritzy sneeze. ☐	
Ziggy sells polka-dot pants. ☐ Ziggy sells big, hot pretzels. ☐	
Alex plays with the fuzzy yellow cat. ☐ That yelling bothers Alex a lot! ☐	
Tony bakes a yummy dish with cheese and egg yolks. ☐ Tony mixes egg yolks and milk for a yummy cake. ☐	
Digging clams in the sun makes Lizzy dizzy. ☐ Lizzy yells for quiet so she can doze. ☐	
Zelda yanks a doll with fuzzy hair out of the bag. ☐ The doll thinks Zelda has a fuzzy beard. ☐	
The Swiss jazz singer is yodeling. ☐ The musical deer wants to be a jazz singer. ☐	

Write it, using a word with *x*, *y*, or *z*.

	______________________
	______________________
	______________________
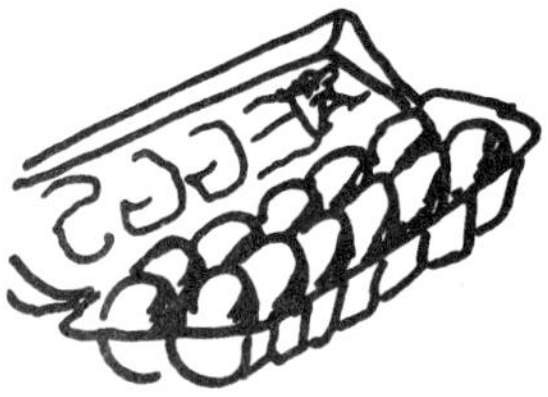	______________________
	______________________
	______________________
	______________________

Lesson 5

Words with *qu*.

Read, write, and ◯ it.

Word			
quacking ________________			
quiz ________________			
liquid ________________			
quart ________________			
squash ________________			
queen ________________			
squid ________________			

the word that matches the picture.

equip or equal?	quart or quarter?
quickly or quicksand?	squash or squint?
quiet or quite?	squeezing or squeaking?
queen-size or quarrel?	square or quail?
liquid or equal?	quoting or quartet?

	Spell.				Write.
	quar	qu	rel	ret	______
2-2=0	o	e	qual	quart	______
25¢	cat	quart	est	er	______
	squee	squeak	y	ty	______
	equip	kin	tet	ment	______
	squeal	ski	ing	ish	______
	squeez	squeal	ing	zit	______

Yes or no?

	Yes	No
Can a blind pig squeal?	☐	☐
Can you squeeze a lemon?	☐	☐
Is oatmeal a liquid?	☐	☐
Can you get equipment from a squid?	☐	☐
Are you acquainted with the queen?	☐	☐
Does a quarter equal twenty-five pennies?	☐	☐
Can you go on a quiz show and win?	☐	☐

the word that matches the picture.

quest quarrel guests	squint sprint squall
quickness equally quietness	quick-witted quarterback quartet
sliver quiver river	quilt wilts stilts
squid squad square	squashy squarely squeaky
quickly quiz grizzly	quail quart quote

Pick the best word to finish each sentence.

liquids	squeezing	squeak
quest	square	equal
quarter	squash	quart

I can drink a ____________________ of milk a day.

Lemonade and rubbing alcohol are both ____________________ .

A pack of gum costs a ____________________ .

Jo is ____________________ the water out of the mop.

Twelve eggs ____________________ one dozen.

Can you hear the wagon wheels ____________________ ?

I hate all kinds of ____________________ and spinach.

X it.

Mabel has three more bananas. ☐ Three plus three equals six. ☐	
The rusty pot was quickly taken off the stove. ☐ Rusty adds a quart of liquid to the pot. ☐	
The queen invites the twins to see the dragon. ☐ The twins own the queerest-looking pet. ☐	
Raymond hopes to squash the big bug. ☐ Rosemond fixes a big squash dish. ☐	
The sheep sleep quietly in the hills. ☐ Bo-Peep quietly gathers her sheep. ☐	
Ruby prints her name on her quiz. ☐ Ruth squeals as she sprints along. ☐	
Sal squints at the grade on her quiz. ☐ Sal's class will have a quick quiz next week. ☐	

Write it, using a word with *qu*.

	______________________
2-2=0	______________________
25¢	______________________
	______________________
	______________________
	______________________
	______________________

Lesson 6

Words with *thr, shr,* and *scr.*

Read, write, and ◯ it.

throwing ____________			
scream ____________			
shrink ____________			
shredded wheat ____________			
scrap heap ____________			
scrub brush ____________			
thrilling ____________			

◯ the word that matches the picture.

	Spell.				Write.
	thru	throw	ish	ing	______________
	scrub	sub	bush	brush	______________
	scratch	thatch	ing	ist	______________
	scra	scram	ping	sing	______________
	scrap	scrape	set	book	______________
	dream	scream	ing	ish	______________
	thrill	shrill	est	ing	______________

Yes or no?

	Yes	No
Will you put a scrapbook on the scrap heap?	☐	☐
Do you scream on a thrilling roller coaster ride?	☐	☐
Do you like shredded wheat with cream and sugar?	☐	☐
Do you use a scraper to take frost off a window?	☐	☐
Will you clean the shrubbery with a scrub brush?	☐	☐
Is your puppy dog scratching fleas?	☐	☐
Can you throw away a sore throat?	☐	☐

◯ the word that matches the picture.

shred shrill shake	scratch screech scrunch
three-color threesome three-decker	scrimp script screen
thatching scratching stitching	scrapbook scaring screen
shrine shrunk shrimp	shingle shrink shred
shrink wrap streamers steamship	shredded wheat shrub shivering

Pick the best word to finish each sentence.

throwing	thrilling	scrambled
sore throat	scrapbook	shrivel
scrub brush	shrink	scraping

You need to do lots of ________________ to remove peeling paint.

It's fun to keep snapshots and things in a ________________ .

You clean the steps with soap and a ________________ .

Do not use hot water when you wash the dress as it may ________________ .

I like ________________ eggs with toast and bacon on Sundays.

You can't sing when you have a ________________ .

Miss June is ________________ away the rubbish.

X it.

Rolf scrambles up the steps and slides down.	☐	
Patsy slid on the steps and fell on Rolf.	☐	
Jaden throws the box of stuff into the scrap bin.	☐	
Jaden scraped his leg on the scrap bin.	☐	
Tisha screams as the bats attack her home.	☐	
Trish screams when the insect stings her leg.	☐	
Sara is watching Ty scratch his back.	☐	
Su Lin is scratching Tigger under the chin.	☐	
Will you shrink in fear if the beast roars?	☐	
Beezy shrank in fear as the bees came near.	☐	
It was thrilling to win the Golden Cup.	☐	
It was thrilling to take a roller coaster ride.	☐	
Dad likes to play squash before going to work.	☐	
Flo is scraping the weeds and vines off the squash plants.	☐	

Write it, using a word with *thr, shr,* or *scr.*

Lesson 7

Words with *spl, spr,* and *str.*

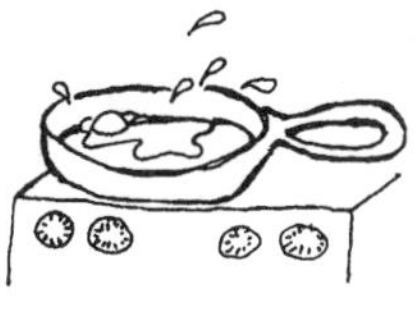

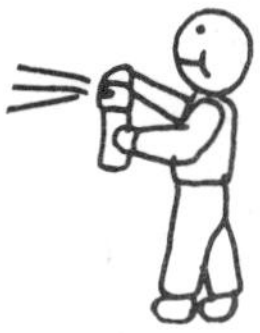

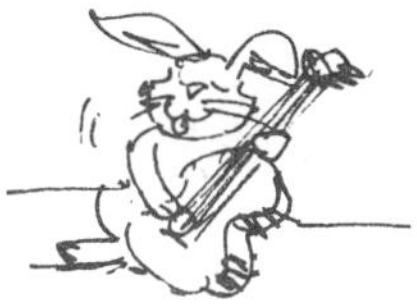

Read, write, and ◯ it.

splendid ________________	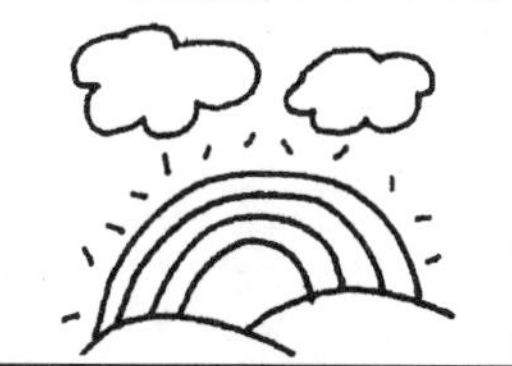	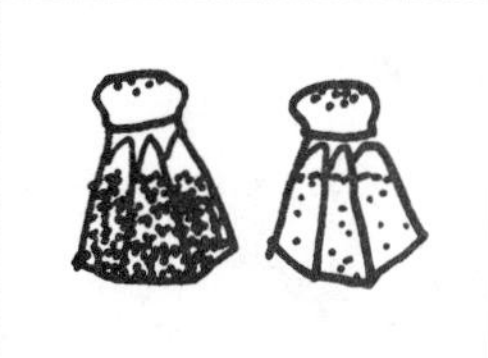	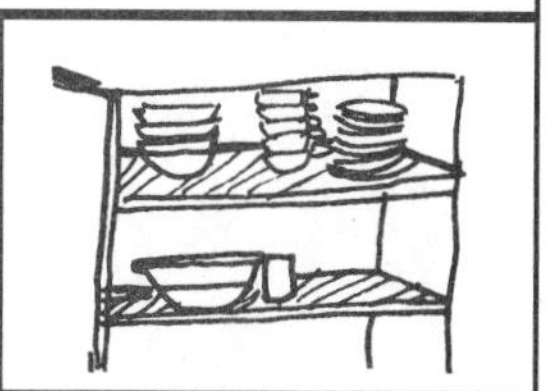
strap ________________	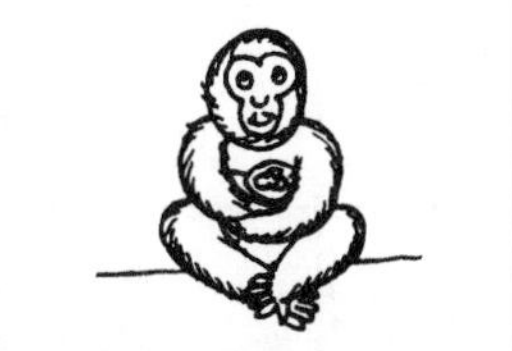	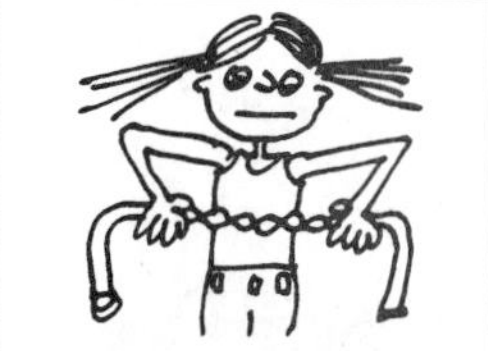	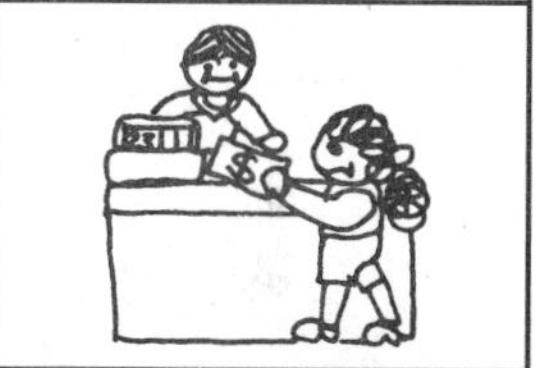
struck ________________	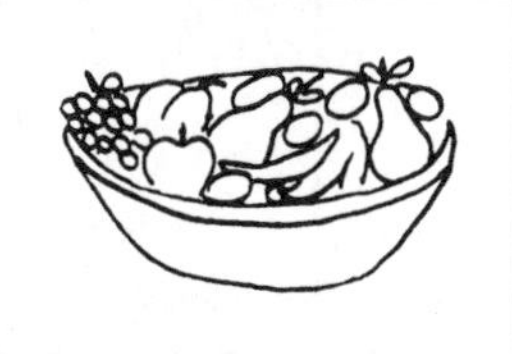	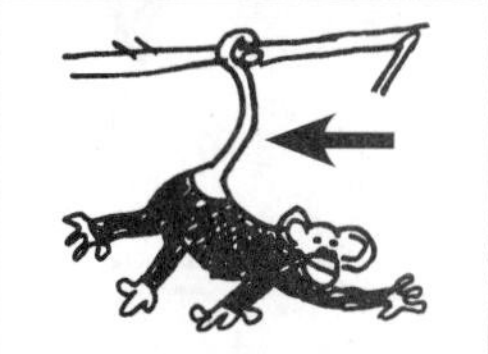	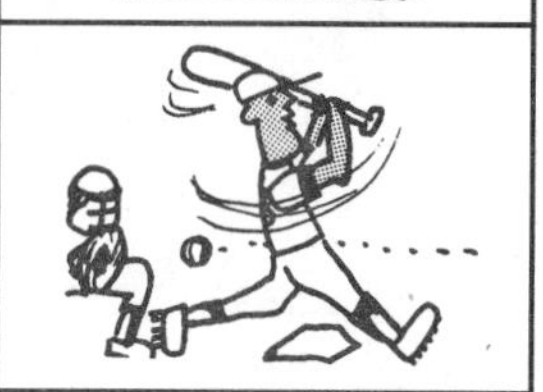
stream ________________	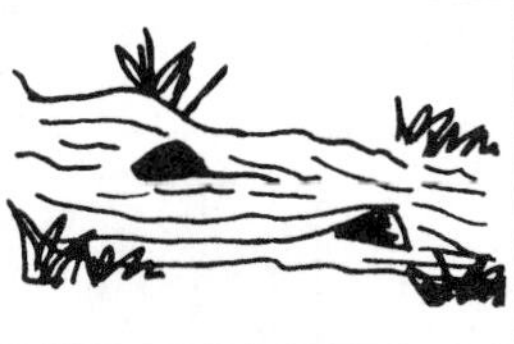	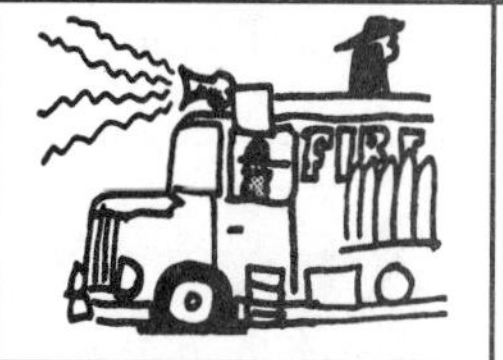	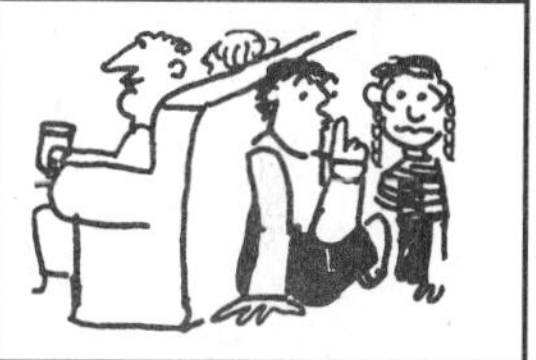
strength ________________	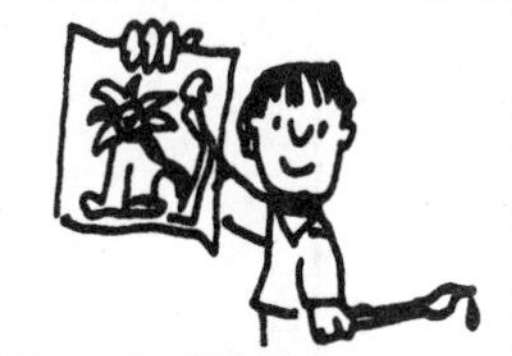	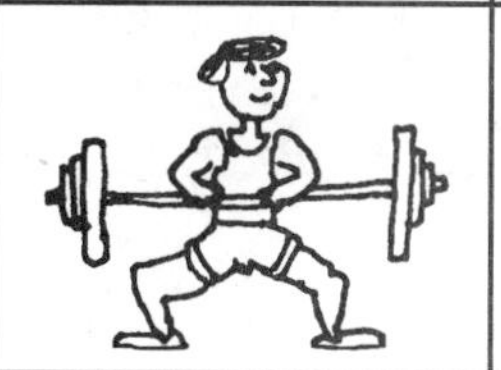	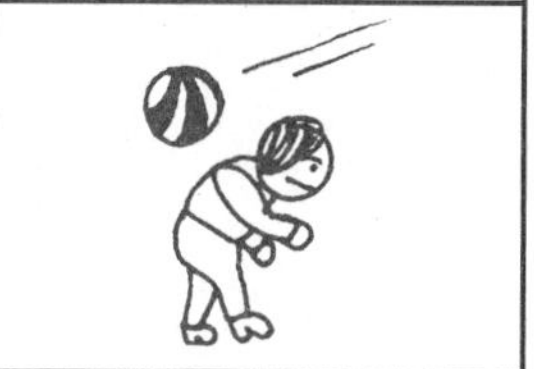
stretch ________________	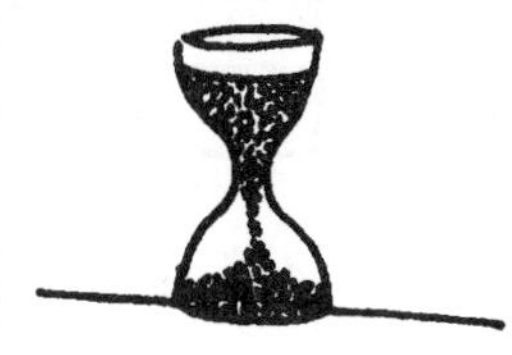	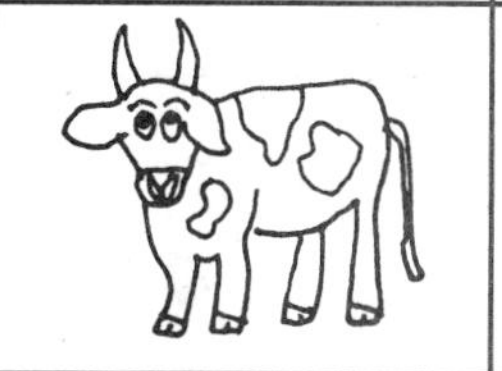	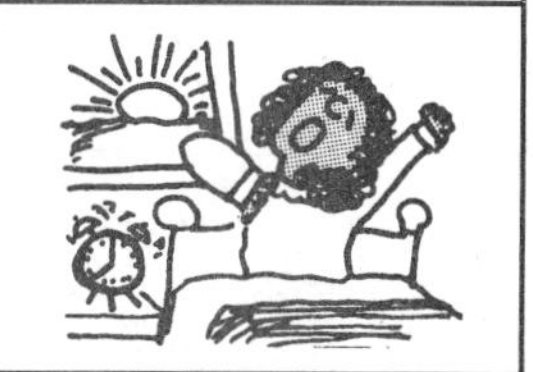
stroking ________________	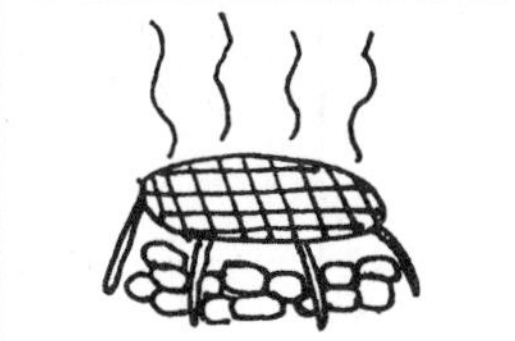	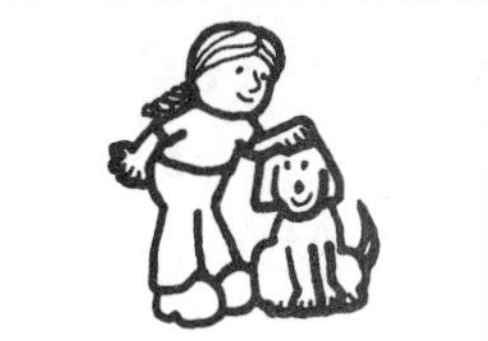	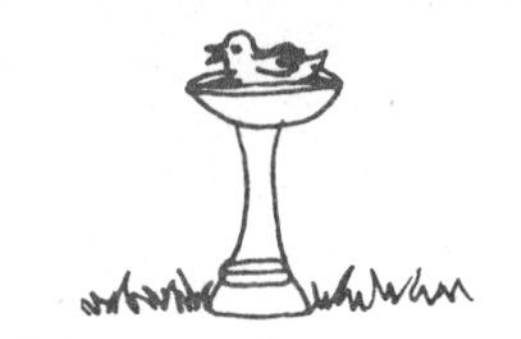

◯ the word that matches the picture.

	Spell.				Write.
	stretch	stick	er	less	______________
	sprig	sprin	kle	gle	______________
	strum	stum	ming	ment	______________
	splat	spit	ten	ter	______________
	stray	spray	can	gan	______________
	stum	strug	gle	ble	______________
	splen	splash	ing	est	______________

Yes or no?

	Yes	No
Can you strum a tune on a banjo?	☐	☐
Can you test your strength?	☐	☐
Can you use a strap to hold bags down?	☐	☐
Will you use a spray can for stripping paint?	☐	☐
Can you straddle a stretcher?	☐	☐
Is it splendid to strike out in a baseball game?	☐	☐
Will dry paint splatter?	☐	☐

◯ the word that matches the picture.

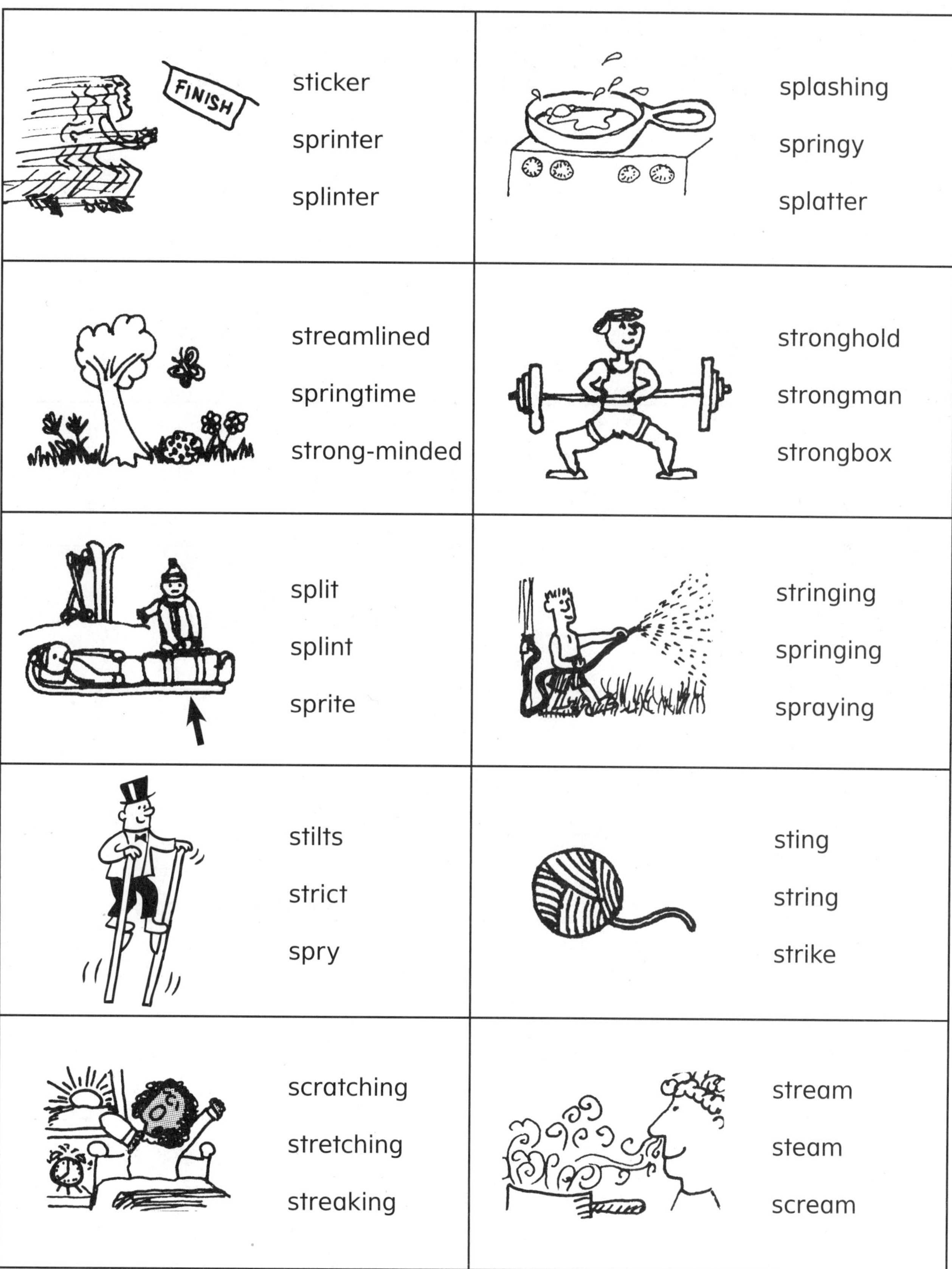

sticker sprinter splinter	splashing springy splatter
streamlined springtime strong-minded	stronghold strongman strongbox
split splint sprite	stringing springing spraying
stilts strict spry	sting string strike
scratching stretching streaking	stream steam scream

Pick the best word to finish each sentence.

string	splatter	stream
splinter	splendid	struggle
stretch	struck	straps

Lulu's backpack has strong ________________ to hold it.

It is best to ________________ before sprinting five miles.

A sunny day is a ________________ time to go hiking.

Rowena came up to bat, but she ________________ out.

Grease will ________________ if the frying pan is too hot.

A yo-yo moves up and down on a ________________ .

It is fun to catch fish or frogs in a shallow ________________ .

X it.

Rita throws a tantrum when Rudy will not play.	☐	
Rudy throws a fast ball and Rita strikes at it.	☐	
Rover hopes to catch striped bass in the stream.	☐	
The striped bass are steaming in the hot oven.	☐	
Tilly can't play with Toto until she stops splashing.	☐	
Tito can't play this spring as his leg is in a cast.	☐	
Rose blasts off in her super, streamlined jet.	☐	
Jeb blasts Rose for not asking him to supper.	☐	
Candy is clapping for the splendid seal act.	☐	
Sal is splendid as she sings and strums her cane.	☐	
Cliff watches as Clem springs off the diving board.	☐	
Clem won the sprint for his team.	☐	
Rudy is splashing as he teaches Cleo to swim.	☐	
Cleo is teaching her pup not to jump up or splash.	☐	

Write it, using a word with *spr, spl,* or *str.*

	____________________
	____________________
	____________________
	____________________
	____________________
	____________________
	____________________

Lesson 8

The ending *-ed* usually means that something has already happened.
-ed says /ĕd/ as in *add<u>ed</u>.*

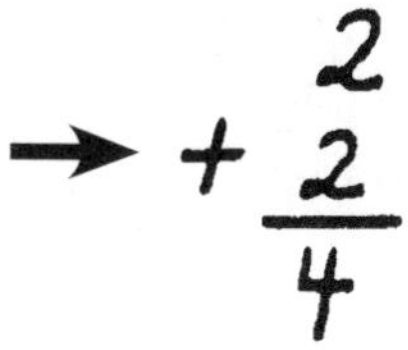

$$\begin{array}{r} 2 \\ \to + \; 2 \\ \hline 4 \end{array}$$

Read, write, and ⬭ it.

posted ____________		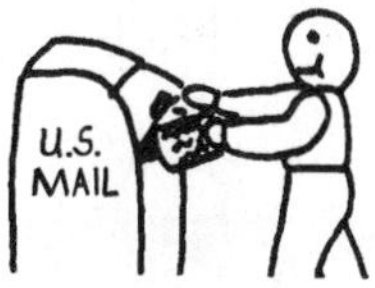 U.S. MAIL	
stranded ____________		 MA'S HOM PLAC	
twisted ____________			
halted ____________			
jolted ____________			
melted ____________			
squinted ____________			

(circle) the word that matches the picture.

posted or pasted?	toasted or twisted?
stranded or scolded?	malted or melted?
speeded or squinted?	wasted or waded?
heated or landed?	quoted or floated?
sprinted or squinted?	mended or molded?

	Spell.		Write.
	salt sal	ed er	________
	squint sprint	er ed	________
	mill roast	ed en	________
	mend mind	ed ted	________
	cold scold	ed de	________
	halt shell	ed red	________
	jolt heat	ed er	________

Yes or no?

	Yes	No
Can you be stranded on a lonely island?	☐	☐
Are roasted peanuts as good as salted popcorn?	☐	☐
Can an email be posted with a stamp?	☐	☐
Could you be blinded by the sunshine?	☐	☐
Is shredded wheat and pickles a tasty treat?	☐	☐
Can a baby be quieted by screaming?	☐	☐
Will you be scolded for going directly to jail and not passing "GO?"	☐	☐

◯ the word that matches the picture.

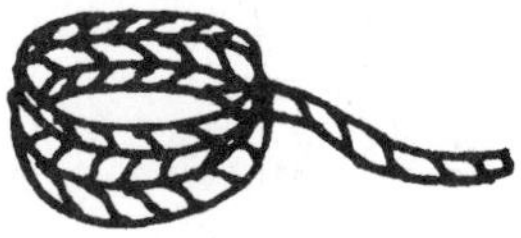 unwinding fair-minded unkindness	 bolted jolted malted
 melted budded salted	 printed sprinted skated
 acquainted adopted aircraft	 squinted skidded subtracted
 mended stunted wilted	 landed loaded lasted
 blasted quilted quieted	 repainted refolded gold-filled

Pick the best word to finish each sentence.

posted	sprinted	halted
squatted	heated	twisted
acquainted	scolded	mended

I put on my sneakers and ____________________ to the mall.

The vines ____________________ over the branches of the tree.

The mail is so slow; this letter was ____________________ three weeks ago.

We put the tea kettle on the stove and ____________________ water for tea.

The cop ____________________ every car making a left turn.

There was a hole in the costume that needed to be ____________________ .

Sasha and I became ____________________ last year when we met in Denver.

X it.

The toad was stranded on a raft in the pond. ☐ Toad was standing with a raft on top of him. ☐	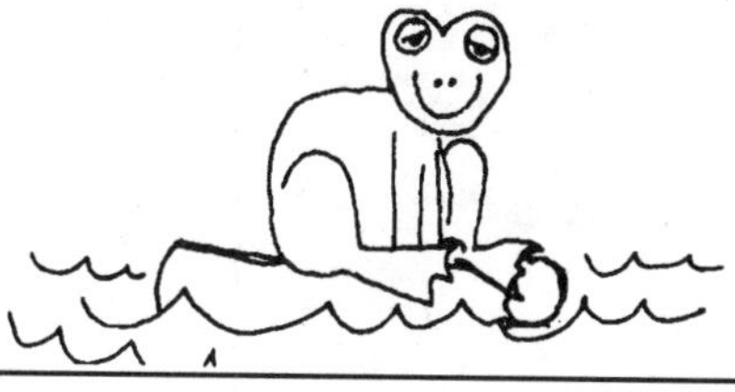
Hilda lifted the stairs with her hands and feet. ☐ The stairs lifted Hilda up to the sky. ☐	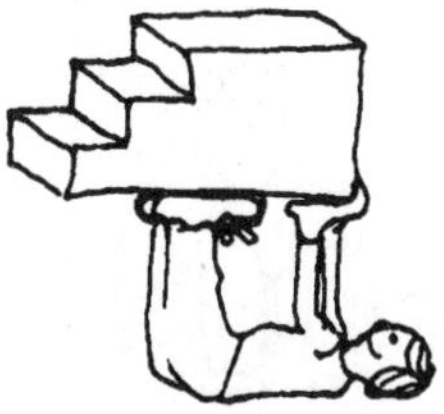
Rover squinted at his strong chain. ☐ Rover squatted down on the velvet chair. ☐	
The sheep scolded Liza for planting seeds. ☐ Liza is acquainted with Shep Sheep. ☐	
Rachel left the dock and is carefully sailing away. ☐ Rachel lifted the lock carefully. ☐	
Robin's plane has landed safely. ☐ The robin landed safely and folded its wings. ☐	
Chet's socks are on his head. ☐ Chet handed his sister the pair of socks. ☐	

Write it, using *-ed* at the end.

Lesson 9

Sometimes *-ed* says /t/ as in *jump*<u>*ed*</u>.

Read, write, and ◯ it.

shopped ____________			
stretched ____________			
dumped ____________			
quacked ____________			
squeaked ____________			
striped ____________			
yipped ____________			

(circle) the word that matches the picture.

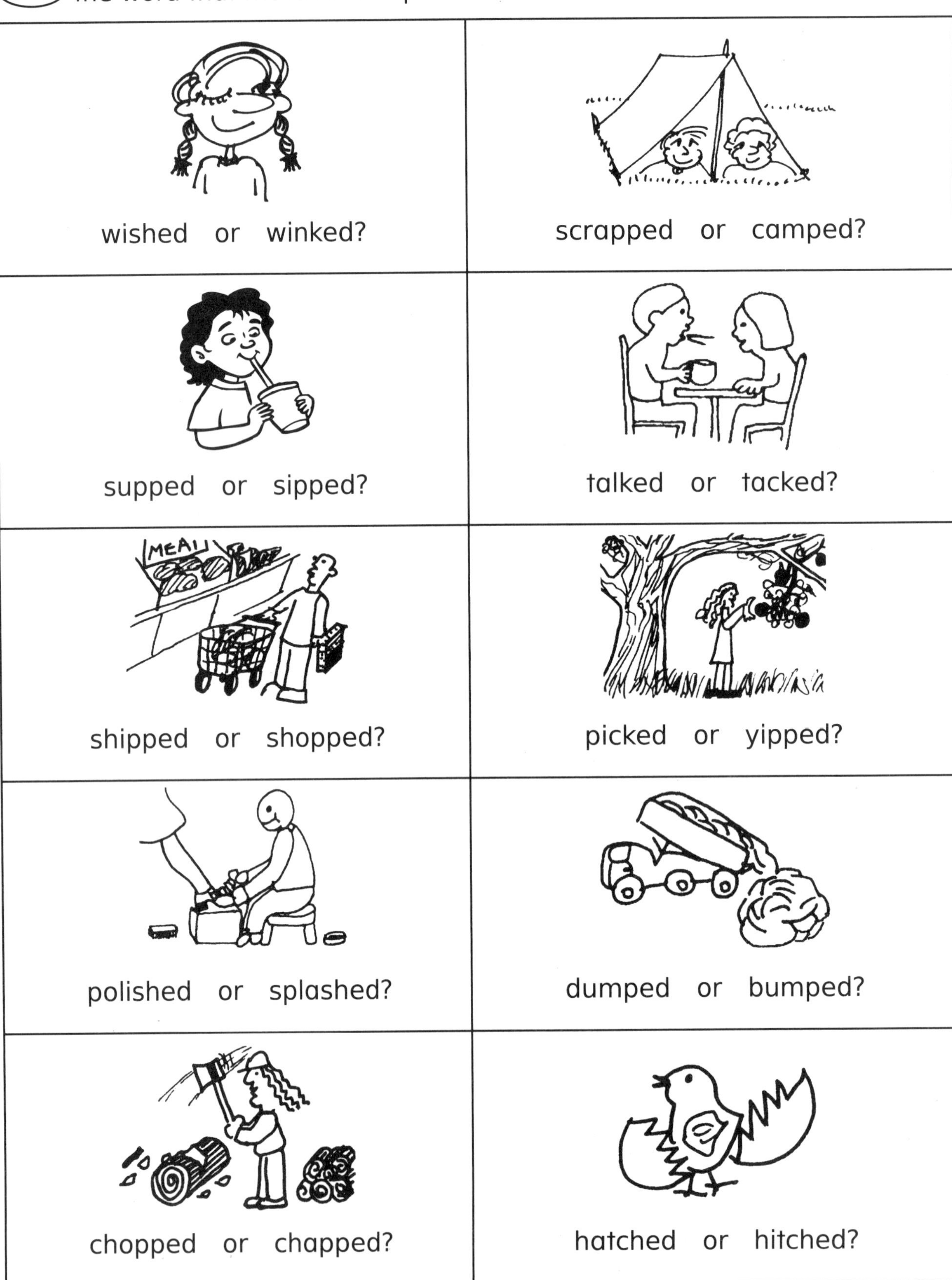

wished or winked?	scrapped or camped?
supped or sipped?	talked or tacked?
shipped or shopped?	picked or yipped?
polished or splashed?	dumped or bumped?
chopped or chapped?	hatched or hitched?

	Spell.		Write.
	strap sipped	milk less	______
	slopped chopped	nuts log	______
	camped capped	zed out	______
	pumped shopped	pen up	______
	wick winked	ted eye	______
	brushed washed	dog hair	______
	locked licked	up pop	______

Yes or no?

	Yes	No
Is a zebra black- and white-striped?	☐	☐
Can a rubber band be stretched?	☐	☐
Have you ever wished for roller blades?	☐	☐
Would the man in the moon have winked at you?	☐	☐
Have you ever walked across a long lake?	☐	☐
Do you get splashed when you have a shore dinner?	☐	☐
Are your jogging sneakers a matched pair?	☐	☐

◯ the word that matches the picture.

 washed swished wished	 pushed punched pinched
 hatched matched mashed	 quicker quaked quacked
 untapped unsnapped unwrapped	 scratched stretched thatched
 chopped shopped shipped	 zipped yipped whipped
 screeched scratched stretched	 splashed slashed smashed

Pick the best word to finish each sentence.

camped	shopped	squeaked
polished	yipped	hatched
dumped	striped	quacked

My pal and I ________________ in a tent near a lake.

The truck ________________ sand on the slippery road.

Weezy ________________ for snow tires for her truck.

The old, rusty door ________________ when you opened it.

Rufus ________________ to be let outside.

The ducks ________________ as they landed on the pond.

Quentin has a red and black ________________ jacket.

X it.

The steamship picked up the tuna fish.	☐	
The tuna fish picked up the live bait.	☐	
Dave talked with the snail about voting.	☐	
The snake told Dave not to vote.	☐	
Foxy winked as he rode the pony.	☐	
Dale wished she could ride like Foxy.	☐	
The tide was not in, so Randy stopped to dig clams.	☐	
Randy stopped by to find out the time.	☐	
The kids chased the kite a long way.	☐	
The kite chased the sun away all day.	☐	
Ziggy yipped as he planted the bone.	☐	
The boat rocked, so Bea decided to go home.	☐	
Nada brushed her hair as she rode the trapeze.	☐	
Nada shopped for rolls and hot cross buns.	☐	

Write it, using a word with *-ed* at the end.

	______________________
	______________________
	______________________
	______________________
	______________________
	______________________
	______________________

Lesson 10

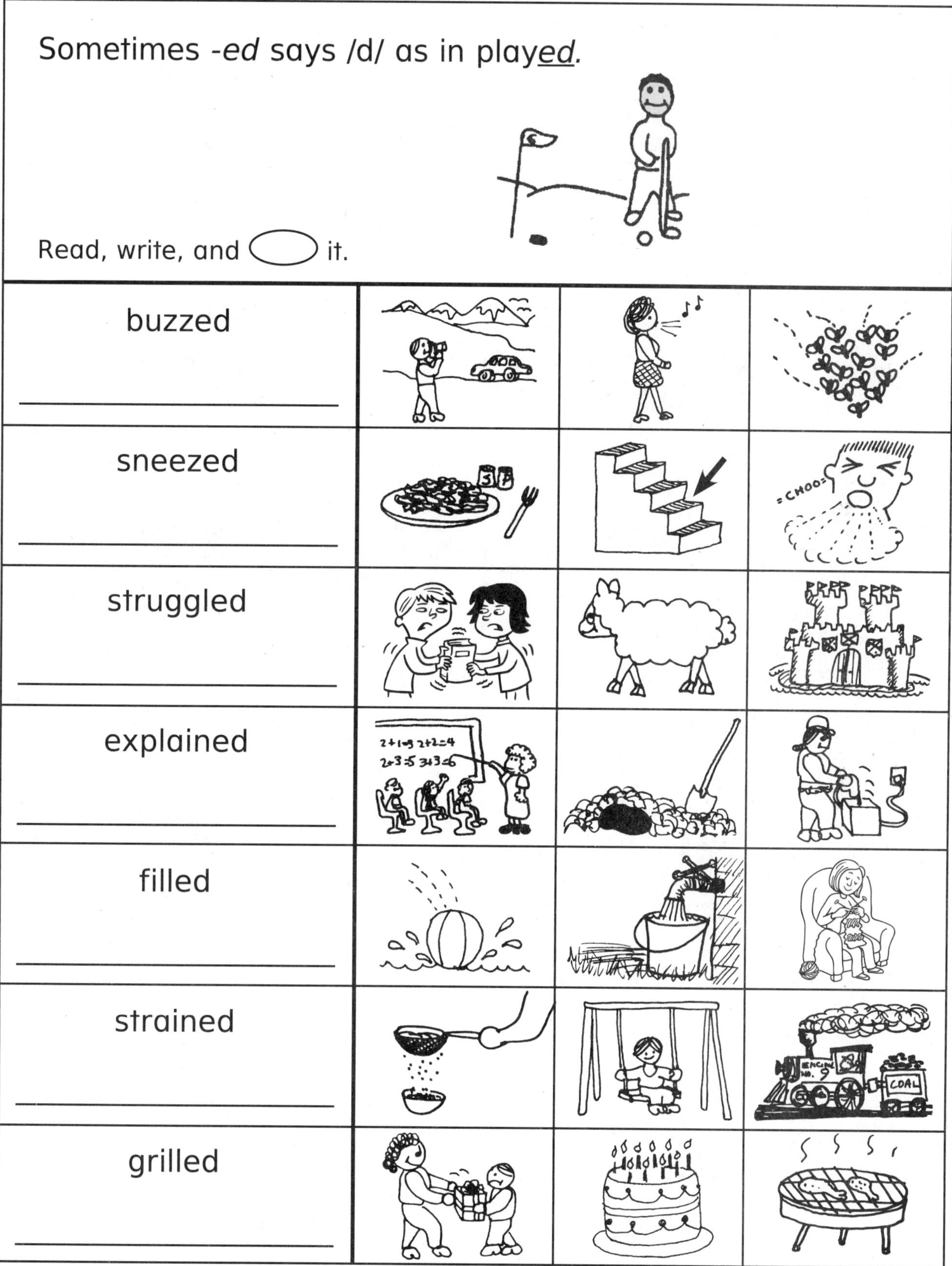

Sometimes *-ed* says /d/ as in play<u>*ed*</u>.

Read, write, and ◯ it.

buzzed ____________			
sneezed ____________			
struggled ____________			
explained ____________			
filled ____________			
strained ____________			
grilled ____________			

◯ the word that matches the picture.

	Spell.		Write.
	played grayed	on swings in bath	______________
	ball plowed	suds snow	______________
	entered explained	map lesson	______________
	box bees	buzzed beaded	______________
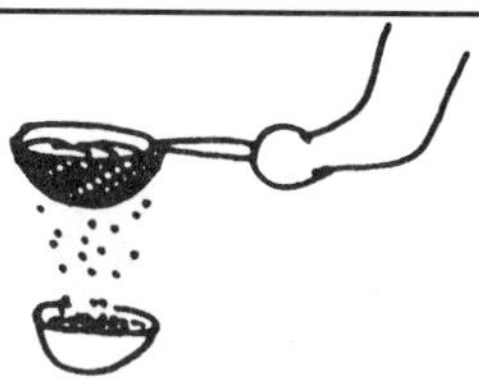	strained stained	beets bets	______________
	sneezed snaz	a lot boat	______________
	gilled grilled	meat mat	______________

Yes or no?

	Yes	No
Have you filled a basket with water?	☐	☐
Has the teacher explained the lesson well?	☐	☐
Have you ever struggled with a big problem?	☐	☐
Are steamed potatoes with butter yummy?	☐	☐
Do you like strained prunes?	☐	☐
Has a supersonic jet skimmed the sky?	☐	☐
Have you ever had a drink that fizzed in the glass?	☐	☐

◯ the word that matches the picture.

 expected expelled explained	 leaned cleaned dreamed
 rambled scrambled eggs scribbling	 clammed slammed slimmed
 squeezed screeched sneezed	 spilled grilled spelled
 yelled quizzed quoted	 limped lifted licked
 homestretch unbuttoned untrimmed	 brushed dozed buzzed

Pick the best word to finish each sentence.

explained	prayed	excused
filled	grilled	buzzed
sneezed	fizzed	strained

The grapes must be ____________________ when you make jelly.

The bees ____________________ all around the hives.

Mom ____________________ to us why she did not want us to go to the river.

We had ____________________ hot dogs for dinner.

When I got a whiff of the red pepper, I ____________________ three times.

Bonita ____________________ her coat pocket with chestnuts.

The teacher ____________________ me from classes to go to the dentist.

X it.

Tilly tapped her toe as she played jazz. Tilly trapped a toad in her playpen.	☐ ☐	
Rozell showed the class its progress. Rozell and the class showed off their costumes.	☐ ☐	
Teddy's jacket was belted with pockets. Teddy wished his jacket fit better.	☐ ☐	
The fattest rat tipped the scales. The fattest rat tossed out the fish scales.	☐ ☐	
Patsy sprinted down to see the truck. Pancho squinted to see what was in the trunk.	☐ ☐	
Donna wished for and got a 10-speed bike. Donna sprinted along behind Betsy's bike.	☐ ☐	
Rosco hated to go for a stroll. Rosco looked at himself and smiled.	☐ ☐	

Write it, using a word that ends with *-ed*.

Lesson 11 • Review Lesson

Read, write, and ◯ it.

rowed ______			
danced ______			
split ______			
polka-dotted ______			
behind ______			
quiet ______			
licked ______			

(Circle) the word that matches the picture.

washed or wished?	daisy or dozed?
chomped or camped?	squid or square?
strength or stamped?	thrifty or throw?
steamed or streamed?	scrapbook or scramble?
pumped or dumped?	checked or cheered?

	Spell.				Write.
	past	post	pox	box	______
	wa	weed	ed	ded	______
	squak	squeak	chy	y	______
	wul	wal	rus	rush	______
	pret	prit	zel	zele	______
	sketch	stretch	ing	er	______
	qui	quick	ded	et	______

Yes or no?

	Yes	No
Will trash be dumped behind a chair?	☐	☐
Does an exam take strength?	☐	☐
Can a squeaky wheel be greased?	☐	☐
Is a baked pretzel salty?	☐	☐
Will a quartet remain quiet?	☐	☐
Are polka-dot overalls snazzy?	☐	☐
Will you waltz with the postman?	☐	☐

◯ the word that matches the picture.

Pick the best word to finish each sentence.

quiet	waltzed	pretzels
squeaky	licked	split
squinted	stumbled	smashed

Felix ____________________ his peppermint candy cane.

Hazel was told to be ____________________ in the old library.

The glass fell and ____________________ on the sidewalk.

We must fix that ____________________ gate.

The postman ____________________ and fell on the sidewalk.

Liza likes salted peanuts and ____________________ .

Ava ____________________ in the sun until she found her sunglasses.

X it.

Lizzy fixed an old wheelchair for Bess. ☐ Lizzy fixed the wheel on the oldest bus. ☐	
Alex finished eating the tub of Swiss cheese. ☐ Alex filled the washtub with Swiss cheese. ☐	
Fritzy sat and waited beside the mailbox. ☐ Fritz fell asleep in the van waiting for the postman. ☐	
Scruffy licked the candy Zack was holding. ☐ Scruffy liked to hold Zack's candy cane. ☐	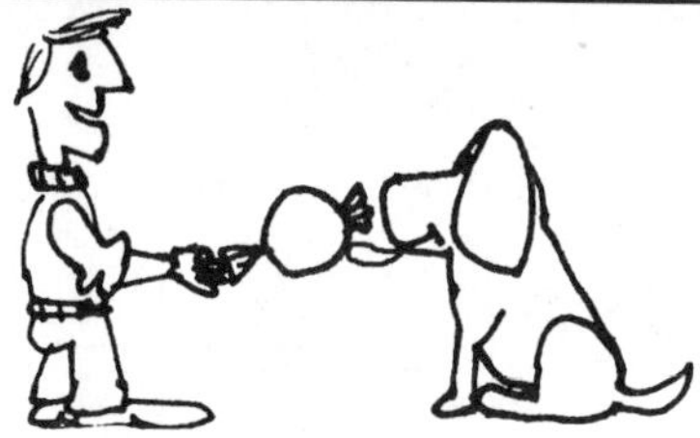
Dez dozed in his comfy bed. ☐ Dez was dizzy from the roller coaster. ☐	
Suzy pitched a thrilling no-hitter. ☐ Suky, the wild pony, is hitched to its halter. ☐	
This crazy insect jumped inside my pants pocket. ☐ That crazy insect camped inside the tent. ☐	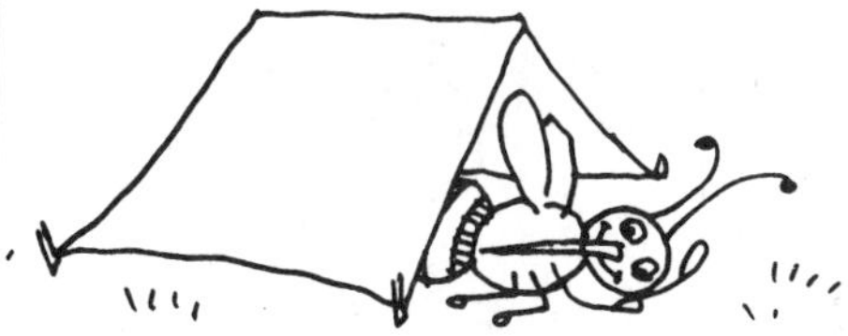

Write it.

	______________________________
U.S. MAIL	______________________________
	______________________________
	______________________________
	______________________________
	______________________________
	______________________________

Book 5½ — Posttest

(Teacher dictated. See Key for Book 5½.)

◯ the word you hear.

1.	mindful moldiest mildness mindless mintiest	2.	goldenrod goldsmith gold dust goldfish goldfinch
3.	expanded expected extended exited expended	4.	kindest kindness unkindness kindliness mankind
5.	zigzagged zoomed zeroed zippered zinger	6.	scaffolding shuffling box holder pot holders scuffling
7.	chartered chalkboard caulking chalked corkboard	8.	postbox postmaster postponed postdated posthaste
9.	screaming screening streaming screeching steaming	10.	fall back fullback backpack rollback quarterback

Book 5½ — Posttest

(Teacher dictated. See Key for Book 5½.)

1. ____

2. ____

3. ____

4. ____

5. ____

6. ____

Book 5½ — Posttest

Read, and then write the word.

1. The green liquid spilled and st________________ my white pants.
2. The kids all sc________________ on the roller coaster ride.
3. One-fourth of a pizza is a qu________________ of it all.
4. I hear my dog sc________________ at the door to come in.
5. I think the tiger is the w________________ animal in the jungle.
6. I got my sleeping bag from the closet and un________________ it.

Book 5½ — Posttest

Use the words to complete the sentences.

Goldilocks	unfolded	goldsmith
told	scolded	folks
coldness	behold	stroller
goldfish	bolted	thread

1. You may remember a folktale about a child named ____________ who went for a stroll and discovered a cute cabin. "I wonder if ____________ live here?" she asked. But no one was there. Goldy began to shiver as the ____________ of the cabin gave her a chill. She ____________ some blankets, slipped into bed, and fell fast asleep. The owners came home, and lo and ____________ ! What did they see? A little gold-haired child sleeping in their bed! They woke Goldy, ____________ her, and ____________ her to go home and never ever come back to that cabin.

walrus	snowfall	tallest
fallen	rolled	wallet
wild	behind	halted

2. One day after a ____________ that was deep and white, I put on my ____________ boots and went for a long beach walk. All of a sudden as came upon the beach, I ____________ as if I had seen a stoplight! There, sunning itself on the frozen shore, was a ____________. I had never before seen a walrus. What a treat to behold! But, as I crept closer, the walrus looked up, saw me, and ____________ back into the sea. Why hadn't I hidden ____________ a tree? I was mad at myself. But I was even madder when I got home and discovered that I had lost my ____________ on my walk. It must have ____________ out of my pocket when I stopped quickly upon seeing that handsome ____________ animal.